HISTORY IN A HURRY

French Revolution

written and drawn by
JOHN FARMAN

MACMILLAN
CHILDREN'S BOOKS

First published 1998 by Macmillan Children's Books
a division of Macmillan Publishers Limited
25 Eccleston Place, London SW1W 9NF
and Basingstoke

Associated companies throughout the world

ISBN 0 330 37089 8

Text and illustrations copyright © John Farman 1998

The right of John Farman to be identified as the
author of this work has been asserted by him in accordance with the
Copyright, Designs and Patents Act 1988.

1 3 5 7 9 8 6 4 2

A CIP catalogue record for this book is available from
the British Library.

Printed and bound in Great Britain
by Mackays of Chatham plc, Kent

⟣ CONTENTS

🗯️ OFF WE GO!

What do you do if your boss, government, king, dictator (or even teacher) is making your life and all your mates' lives impossible, refusing to listen when you complain? You either leave (if they'll let you), or you decide to do something about it. That's what's called a *revolution*. There have been revolutions throughout history and throughout the world (there's probably one going on somewhere right now). In places like South America they still have them practically every day, with a matinée on Sundays – in fact revolting is almost a national sport down that way.

The French Revolution, in the 18th century, was a particularly nasty one, and one which the English sat back and enjoyed from a distance, hearing of their terrible misfortunes, and gloating to their hearts' content (we've always disapproved of the French, almost as much as they've always disapproved of us!).

SERVES 'EM RIGHT –
IF YOU ASK ME

Warning!!!

At this point, I should remind you that the French, being a hot-blooded, passionate people (unlike us lot*) are capable of extreme violence against each other and I reckon their revolution wins just about every World Nastiness prize. I give you fair warning that this little book is not for the faint-hearted: enter at your own peril!

PS. If you notice little comments like the one below dotted throughout the book, that's my editor, Susie, sticking her oar in. Try to ignore her – I do.

* Speak for yourself! Ed

Chapter 1

WHAT? WHY? WHEN? AND WHO?

The causes of all the problems that rocked 18th century France can be traced back for centuries. In a nutshell . . . At that time the French were still quite rich (compared to everyone else), but most of the money was held by very few people. Having said that, the French peasants (there were 26 million of 'em) owned between a quarter and a third of the land – far more than our lot. All the same, they had their work cut out simply to stay alive, as very few individuals owned enough land to support their ever-growing families. Worse than that, they were forced to watch the idle rich swanning around showing little concern for their poorer brothers (apart from trying to trick them out of any land they *did* own). So what? I hear you say – that was always the case and, anyway, isn't that what peasants do – go hungry and complain a lot? But when it comes to complaining, the French take *le biscuit*. Read on . . .

STOP COMPLAINING

Grub Alert

The French have always been famed for their amorous pursuits, but in the 18th century they seemed to be at it all the time – which resulted in a population explosion, believe it or not. Unfortunately, the farmers were at it too; they didn't even have time to produce the extra food needed to feed all those extra little French mouths (36% of the total population of France were under 20). Just as things were getting really bad . . . they suddenly got much worse – when the harvest failed in 1788. Almost overnight, the thousands of starving vagrants who'd been scouring the countryside (and then the towns) for something to keep them alive, turned into bandits. And what do bandits do? Horrid things to anyone that gets in their way!

The Three Estates

Before we go any further, let me briefly describe how French society was carved up. Unlike these days where, in most countries, deciding where one class begins and another ends can be a bit tricky (see New Labour), in France the divisions were clear and everyone knew which side they were on whether they liked it or not.

There were the three main classes, called the Three Estates.

The First Estate: The Clergy

Although the average parish priest was no richer than the poorest of his parishioners, the upper clergy were doing very nicely, thank you. They had little to do with God, but a lot to do with sucking up to the aristocracy and making fortunes from the tithes charged to the tenants of their massive estates. These rich churchmen made up the First Estate.

Useless Fact No. 745

A tithe, by the way, meant that a poor peasant farmer had to give at least 10% of everything he earned or produced from his land to the fat cat who owned it.

The Church had even wheedled its way out of paying any taxes – which meant there was no check on their massive wealth. Church properties, for instance, often made up a large proportion of the town and, as the clergy were the only people who could read, they wielded huge power and influence over the thick peasants.* Just think, they could interpret any shiny new government laws as and how they liked.

The Second Estate: The Nobility

There were tons more noblemen in France than over here, as in Britain it was only the eldest sons who inherited the noble status (and the loot). In France everyone remotely connected to an aristocratic family, even down to favoured servants or pets, could enjoy noble status if it was bestowed upon them.

ARISTOCAT →

---

* Not thick, just uneducated. Ed

The nobility numbered some 400,000, which was just over 1.5% of the population.

Like the upper clergy of the First Estate, the aristocracy also managed to wheedle their way out of paying most of the taxes (and even their debts, come to that) and they also had a stranglehold on all the best jobs.

The French aristocracy were often at odds with royalty (who were above all this Three Estates business anyway) and would have done anything to chip away at their absolute power (which was already going off the boil). To make matters worse, at the bottom end of the nobility, the poor ones were also becoming a trifle nervous about the wealth of the richer merchants and farmers at the top of the Third Estate (coming next).

The Third Estate: The Rest

Anyone else, rich or poor, who hadn't quite managed to squeeze into the First or Second Estates was dumped with 98% of the population (26,000,000) into the Third Estate.

At the top of this Third Estate, any landowner, financier or lawyer who had the necessary readies could shove his family name into the ranks of the nobility by buying a title, or bullying some up-market lad into marrying his daughter (with the added sweetener of quite a lot of money). But when times got rough (which they did, as you'll find out if you read on), these chaps were not to be counted on by their Third Estate brothers, as all they seemed to do was ape those from the upper Estates.

In the middle of this Estate were all the shopkeepers, master craftsmen and their workers and servants, who were always having a go at the farmers, because although their wages stayed the same, food prices (especially bread) went up and down like a yo-yo.*

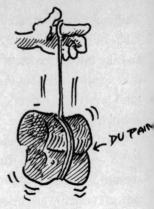

← DU PAIN

The poverty-stricken countryside was a potential battleground. The humble peasant, at the bottom of the Third Estate, continually struggled to pay his tithe to the rich landowners or to the better-off farmers who took the peasants' hard-grown produce in return for lending them the essential implements and livestock. As you can see, it was a bit of a no-win situation for the peasants. And if there was a dodgy harvest, the poor peasant was in even deeper poo as he had to buy grain to live. Those naughty richer farmers would store up grain in times of plenty and then hike up the price when there wasn't much around. The sight of barns brimming over with grain, when the poor old peasant hadn't had any dinner for days, did little for community relations (or the crime rate).

Estate Hate
However much they all needed each other, all the members of all the Estates despised all the other members of all the other Estates.

---

* What's French for yo-yo? Ed
Je ne sais pas. JF

Deep, Deep Debt

By the early part of the
1780s poor old Louis XVI
and his government were
sliding down the slippery slope
into bankruptcy. The government
were spending francs (French money) like
they were going out of fashion, and Louis had to pay not only
the government, but his lawyers and, most of all, his colossal
debts (with interest).

Useless Fact No. 747
In 1788, 50% of all the government's spending was simply paying
off the interest on money they'd borrowed earlier.

Louis realized he could jack up taxation, but there was one
slight snag. Only one of the three Estates paid proper taxes
anyway . . . You've got it – the Third. In other words, those
least able to afford it. His next brainwave was to sell smart
government jobs which brought with them snazzy noble titles
(which would then stay with the family concerned for ever and
ever). In the 18th century, up to 50,000 people were thought to

...ned the French nobility in this way, which, as you can ...gine, really got up the noble noses of the proper old nobility no end.

Poor Lonely Louis

By 1789 the king was at his wits' end – there were hardly any more people to borrow money from. He realized that if he couldn't, it was a dead cert that his government would collapse . . .

So, *mes enfants*, that was basically* the setting for what was to become the most famous and the most bloody revolution of all time.

* How basic can you get? *Ed*
I'm in a hurry. *JF*

* Editorial Interruption *

Er, excuse me, but aren't you going to answer the
questions in your chapter title?
Like: WHAT, WHY, WHEN and WHO? Ed.

Author's Reply

Well, I've answered WHO (peasants vs aristos),
and it's pretty obvious WHY,
and I told you WHEN at the beginning
and the rest of the book will cover WHAT.
So there. JF

But just for the record here are a few more WHYs.

The French were in a period called the Enlightenment
when intellectuals wanted to change almost everything just
for the sake of it.

The Revolution was hugely helped by the weakness of
Louis XVI and his rather lightweight wife, Marie-
Antoinette.

The provincial aristocracy started to question the say-so
of royalty when they began to poke their noses into their
business.

There was a conspiracy by small groups of British Agents
determined to whip up trouble overseas.

Useless and Fictional Fact No. 750

Probably the most famous character from the French Revolution didn't exist at all. The Scarlet Pimpernel was a figment of Baroness Orczy's imagination, and she wrote several books about him. He was supposed to have been a dashing British aristocrat who risked life and limb to save his French mates.

They seek him here,
They seek him there,
Those Frenchies seek him everywhere.
Is he in heaven,
Or is he in hell,
That darned elusive Pimpernel?

Chapter 2

A BIT ABOUT LOUIS XVI

One of the main stars (although presumably he'd have preferred not to be) of the violent soap opera that came to be called the French Revolution, was Louis XVI. Young Louis, from the line of Bourbons (named after the biscuits*) was only 19 when he followed his grandad to the throne in 1774, inheriting the mess resulting from all the injustices dished out by all those fourteen Louises (is that right? Louis's?) who'd gone before him. He was a quiet, modest lad by all accounts, well aware of his own weaknesses, but with a stroppy tongue and wicked temper. Poor Louis was behind the door when looks were handed out, being shortish and overweight and having a wet, flabby mouth and wobbly double chin.

IRRESISTIBLE BISCUIT JOKE!

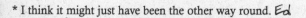

* I think it might just have been the other way round. Ed

Useless Fact No. 753

It was no surprise that Louis was on the tubby side (for *tubby* read *fat*). Breakfast would often consist of 'four cutlets, a chicken, a plateful of ham, half a dozen eggs in a thick meat sauce and a bottle and a half of champagne'. Not a bowl of muesli in sight. By lunchtime he was usually hungry again.

His deportment also left a lot to be desired and, as he shuffled along like an old bear*, he was always tripping over his sword. Like all French royalty, Louis was addicted to hunting but unusually (because most kings were bone idle) had also learned the craft of locksmithery, which, thinking about it, really should have come in useful, as he was to spend quite a bit of his life locked up.

Time for a Wife

At 15 he married the soon-to-be famous and already beautiful Marie-Antoinette, the 14-year-old 15th

daughter of the Emperor Francis and Empress Maria Theresa of Austria, who'd given birth to her in an armchair, which indicates that the marriage just might have been

WILL THERE BE ANYTHING ELSE YOUR MAJESTY?

* Don't be so bear-ist. Ed

more political than anything else.* Louis had never been very good at girls, even when he was the *Dauphin* (pronounced 'Dough-Fan') – the French name for the eldest son of the King. For a start, he'd never got to know any birds of his own age and for a second he had this wacky idea that they robbed a boy's soul (as well as his pocket money).

Useless and Very Boring Fact No. 757

Louis would often spend hours in his closet, telescope in hand, looking out of the window to see who was coming up the drive to the front door at Versailles.

Wedded Bliss (Not)

Louis and Marie-Antoinette had no children in the first few years of their marriage, which might have had something to do with the fact that they didn't get an awful lot of pleasure from each other at bedtime – which might in turn have had something to do with the fact that Louis had a small but embarrassing physical deformity (three guesses . . .). Eventually he had an operation on the 'little royal part' and he and the wife were able to produce three *enfants*. Louis was devoted to his kids and was said to have never really got over the loss of his eldest son, who died of tuberculosis, at the age of eight.

Mind you, if the poor kid had known what was coming, he'd have considered himself lucky, by jove.

---

* Why does being born in an armchair make the marriage political? *Ed*
No, having royal parents, silly! *JF*

Useless Fact No. 760

As Louis got older he became weirder and weirder, playing sub-childish pranks on the servants, like running through the court with his trousers round his ankles (sounds quite a laugh)* and insisting on having a large audience of courtiers when he and his queen ate their meals (in silence). He'd find practically anything to do to avoid facing up to his duties as king.

* I was always worried about you. *Ed*

Chapter 3

A BIT ABOUT MARIE-ANTOINETTE

Being the 15th kid in a family usually means that you don't get much attention (or many presents at Christmas). Marie-Antoinette was no exception. When she finally said goodbye to her family, to take up her arranged and hugely publicized marriage to Louis, she was carried away to a little island on the Rhine, stripped of all her Austrian clothes and symbolically delivered to the French stark naked, chilly and just a trifle upset. She was dead nervous at the wedding, but not nearly as nervous as her poor young hubby, who shook like a leaf and blushed deepest scarlet throughout the ceremony. Most people

SHE'LL DO NICELY

thought Marie-Antoinette bright, vivacious and a right little flirt, but completely unsuited for the job of Queen (26,000,000 French peasants tended to agree). Unfortunately, being the last in the line, her education was practically non-existent – and it was said that even when grown-up her writing was worse than a child's and her speling atroshus.

Dull Routine

Poor Marie was terrified of being bored and found court life stuffy to the point of stuffocation.* Allow me to present a typical day in the early part of her marriage to the *Dough-Fan* (before she was Queened), loosely translated from a letter to her mum.

9.00 am:	Get out of bed, and call the servants to dress me. A ridiculous protocol occurs. My underwear usually has to be handed to me by my *dame d'honneur*, but if there are others of higher rank in the room, it must be passed round in order of seniority, while I stand shivering in the corner. In the absence of morning telly or radio, I then kneel by the bed and say prayers (like 'Lord, get me out of here').
10.00 am:	Time for breakfast [*French toast?*]
10.35 am:	Go round to visit my aunts who live in another part of the palace and meet my husband – who has a separate apartment. It's such a drag – everywhere I go, I have to be followed by courtiers and hangers-on.

* Stuffocation? Ed

11.00 am: Personal hairdresser arrives to fix and powder my personal hair (or wig if I'm having a bad-hair day).

11.30 am: Call everyone in to watch and chat while I have my make-up put on. Then I show the guys the door before I slip into my proper dress in front of *les girls*.

12.00 am: Time for Mass with husband Louis.

12.30 pm: Back for lunch with hubby, usually in silence, in front of anyone who cares to watch.

1.30 pm: Lunch over, return to either his apartment or mine. Work (again) on the embroidered waistcoat for Louis' grandad – the King. [*It took the poor dear years to complete.*]

3.00 pm: Visit the aunts again.

4.00 pm: Time for boring old lessons. I think my teacher, the Abbé Vermont, fancies me.

I THINK I'M GOING TO HAVE TO KEEP YOU IN AFTER LESSONS

5.00 pm:	Music time. Music master arrives and I practise on the clavicle* for an hour (yawn).
6.00 pm:	Go round yet again to the aunts, with Louis.
7.00 pm:	Play cards and usually win.
8.00 pm:	Take supper with aunts and sometimes husband. He goes out most nights, leaving me at home.
9.00 pm:	Read for a bit and then sleep on sofa till the king arrives.
11.00 pm:	Go to bed, ready for exactly the same routine tomorrow.

And you think your life's boring!

Marie Breaks Out

Marie-Antoinette later grew to despise the court and its stuffy ways and was always seen to be doing the wrong thing at the wrong time. If she felt like laughing at a particularly sombre occasion she'd let fly, to the disapproval of all those around her. If she suddenly felt like chucking her hat in a lake – she did. She'd also tease poor Louis mercilessly in front of the court, and break just about every law of etiquette there was to break, including the one which said it was demeaning for a woman to applaud at the opera. When it came to getting around, she found the palace coachmen far too slow and tedious, preferring to tear about in her own sports cabriolet at breakneck speed. She became a notorious tomboy, often ignoring the fine fashions of the court in favour of plain muslin. At other times, however, she would spend a fortune on clothes, often buying several magnificent frocks and ludicrous

---

* I think you might mean a *clavichord* (early piano). A clavicle is a collar-bone. Ed

towering head-dresses every week
– before sending her poor
husband, who was broke
anyway, the bill.

THEY'RE NOT HAVING ANY OF MY CAKE!

Useless Fact No. 763
Marie has gone down in history for the comment 'Then let them eat cake' – that she was supposed to have made on hearing that the peasants had no bread to eat. She never said it.

Extravagance

The poor French poor hated poor Marie mostly for the huge amount of money she got through. At the height of their disapproval, she retreated to her own little palace, the Palais du Petit Trianon, a wee gift from the king. There she had all the grounds changed to the style of an English garden (*très* posh) at a cost of 150,000 *livres**, and had her own theatre (only one play was ever presented) and life-size model village built. There, she would sometimes pretend to be a common dairymaid, which she thought a right laugh.

The 'toy' village (eight cottages and a farm) was simply a plaything – a bit like an 18th-century EuroDisney, built to look old and picturesque, right down to painted cracks on the new

* What's a *livre*? Ed
A French pound. JF

walls and designer broken cobblestones. Marie insisted on only the whitest of lambs, the cleanest of cows and the prettiest of milkmaids (my kind of farm), who carried the finest porcelain milk jugs. All this at a time when next door, the hovel-dwelling proper farm labourers were literally starving to death. Tactful, *je ne pense pas*!

Useless Fact No. 766

Although Marie-Antoinette was regarded as beautiful by 18th-century standards, from the pictures I've seen, she would never turn heads these days, having a rather odd, dome-like forehead and a very weak chin. That's in-breeding for you (Windsors take note).

Chapter 4

DISASTER LOOMS

The Big Powers

The map of central Europe looked a bit different in the 18th century to how it does now and all the different players were continually at each other's throats.

THIS LOOKS A BIT DIFFERENT *

EUROPE

At the top bit, bordering Poland and the Holy Roman Empire, in what is now Northern Germany, was Prussia, ruled by the fearsome Frederick the Great, who was an absolute monarch (which meant he didn't have to take a blind bit of notice of what anyone else told him).

* Extremely helpful, Mr Farman. Ed
I told you I hate doing maps. JF.

The Habsburgs (or Hapsburgs) ruled another big empire (called, surprisingly, the Habsburg Empire) up that way, which included Austria, Hungary and the Austrian part of the Netherlands. Their boss was Emperor Joseph II, another absolute monarch. This empire, however, was all over the shop and so divided that its people spoke no less than twenty different languages (not each person, I hasten to add).

Russia was a huge primitive country ruled by the mighty Peter and Catherine the Great(s) (also absolute monarchs). It had nicked vast areas from Sweden, Poland and Turkey.

Down below, in Southern Europe, was the mighty Ottoman Empire which had all the countries round the Black Sea including Turkey, Greece and Hungary. (More absolute monarchs.)

Britain, bless her, was all on her own, extremely comfortably off and a powerful force in the world (those were the days, eh?). Maybe its success was due to the fact that our king, George III, had to do as his parliament told him – the opposite of an absolute monarch. Either way, Britain had a sizeable empire of its own and was far more advanced, industrially-speaking, than anyone else.

Meanwhile, Back at *Le Ranch*

I suppose, as this book's about the French Revolution, I ought to concentrate on the French.*

In 1780 France had a population three times that of Britain. Their government was in big-time financial trub, having lost most of its territories to Britain in the Seven Years War and having bloodied its nose in the American War of Independence. As a result the French ministers borrowed vast amounts of francs in an effort to keep all their economic balls in the air (to use a juggling expression). By 1785 France was as good as broke, and Louis and his ministers sussed that, if they didn't tighten their belts pretty *tout de suite*, they'd go under – and how!

But government cuts could only go so far – then, as I mentioned before, it was up to the people . . . they'd simply have to pay more taxes. Ah yes, but maybe not *all* the people. The noble powers-that-be (or were) thought they'd limit it to just the poor old Third Estate, who immediately spotted what a swizz this was and demanded (with menaces and grimaces) that the other two Estates put their well-manicured hands in their well-tailored pockets too.

This was easier said than done, as Louis, the last in a long line of monarchs with absolute power, had lost a lot of said power to the nobility, who weren't about to be told what to do.

* About time too. Ed.

Down Le Plughole

I've already talked about the bad harvests in chapter 1, but these were combined with a severe economic plunge. People just weren't buying French no more. By the end of the decade everyone, from the bottom of the Third Estate to the top of the Second, had had enough and riots were breaking out all over the shop. The chap brought in to try and sort it out was the minister of finance, Charles-Alexandre Calonne, who decided that the only way to get out of the mess was to tax *all* the land including that owned by the two top Estates. A sensible move, but asking for trouble. He called a meeting of these two Estates called the Assembly of Notables and tried to convince them that the king really was skint and needed money fast. This, as you can imagine, went down like a submarine with the plug pulled out. In a last-ditch attempt to get out of the . . . mess (for want of a better word), the government called an emergency meeting at Versailles. This was called the 'States General' (the first for 150 years), and it was hoped that representatives of all three Estates might at least try to thrash their way out of the mess.

Louis Bows Out

Louis listened to their whingeing, but became angry and refused to play any more – abandoning the meeting. Actually, he might have been a bit stupid, but he certainly wasn't daft. He knew full well that the nobility wouldn't let him make any reforms so he replaced Calonne with a guy called Brienne, who realized that if he were ever to get this new tax through, he could only do it with the say-so of the *Parlement** de Paris* (the Supreme Court of France). But they – being made up of

* Shouldn't that be *Parliament?* Ed
Not in French, it's not. JF

the nobility – would have none of it, for fairly obvious reasons – so the king sacked the lot of 'em.

Things Get Worse

Louis was now desperate for cash (I know the feeling) and, just to put the tin lid on it, the harvest failed yet again, causing the price of wheat to go through the roof and the now extremely unpleasant peasants to riot.

Louis called another meeting of the States General in 1789, but this time all the better-off members of the Third Estate – magistrates, teachers, bankers, pop stars,* etc. – got it into their heads that they wanted a say in how the country was run – in other words, a piece of the action. Worst of all, they demanded a constitution, or set of rules, that even the king would have to recognize.

It was these changes proposed by the Third Estate that lit the touchpaper of the Revolution.

* Please! Ed

On the Edge

King Louis (surprise, surprise) would have none of this rules business and tried to stop the meeting with the help of the First and Second Estates. The Third Estate were consequently well fed up and formed what they called the National Assembly as a slap in the face and direct challenge to the king. They even asked anyone from the other two Estates to join them if they felt like it. Many, like the Compte de Mirabeau and the Marquis de Lafayette, seeing the writing on their personal walls, did just that, hoping that they might be able to moderate the Revolution that was becoming like a massive spot waiting to be squeezed.*

The day after they'd formed this National Assembly, the representatives of the Third Estate turned up for their usual meeting and found they were locked out and confronted by lots of nasty soldiers. This really hacked them off, so they went to a nearby covered tennis court and had a jolly nice meeting of their own (called, oddly enough, the Meeting of the Covered Tennis Court) in which they swore not to give up until a proper fair government had been formed – and never again to play tennis in the rain.

Clever Louis pretended to accept the new Assembly, despite the fact that he and his noble mates hated the idea. The kunning king kept his fingers krossed and secretly ordered his troops to march on Versailles to deal with these dreadful uppity common folk.

Meanwhile . . .

Elsewhere in the country the atmosphere had become white-hot, as the poor were convinced that the rich, and therefore the

---

* That's really disgusting. Ed
Sorry. How about 'massive boil'? JF

king, were hoarding grain as a way of beating them into submission – which, somewhat surprisingly, they weren't.* It was obvious that the poor would support the new National Assembly. Talk of revolution was thick in the air. Problem was, Louis' army, who were there to stop revolutions, were not that thrilled with their boss either. They hadn't been paid for months and would soon be as hungry as the rest of the people. Why should they obey orders?

Basically, the natives were becoming very restless . . .

* Good idea, though. Ed

☁= *Chapter 5*

☁= *REVOLUTION (AT LAST)*

On the 12th July 1789, Camille Desmoulins, a cross young
Parisian journalist (with a girl's name) brandishing two pistols,
called the people to arms and marched with 8,000 equally
cross citizens straight up to the walls of the Bastille (France's
nastiest prison) where all the weapons were kept. They
smashed down the prison gates, removed all the weapons (and
the governor's head), released the prisoners and marched away
in triumph. Later, the Bastille was torn apart brick by brick.
This symbolized both the overthrow of France's medieval past
and the end of the tyrannical rule of the king.* As news spread
throughout Europe there was a massive joyful outcry from the
Euro-poor, who were so happy that they danced in the streets
(it takes all sorts, I suppose). A few members of the Third
Estate then set up a new government for Paris (called the
Commune). This was a signal for the poor all across France to
pull their fingers out and take matters into their own hands.

La Grande Peur

Outside Paris things were hotting up too. A 'Great Fear' swept
the country, encouraged by a group called the Jacobins
(staunch Revolutionaries). Rumours were rife . . .

Was it true that Marie-Antoinette had attempted to blow
up the Assembly?

---

* Fancy that! Ed

Were there really foreign brigands from England and Spain marching on rural France?

Were foreign powers preparing to invade to restore the king?

Had Polish troops truly landed at Dunkirk?

Did the aristocracy really eat frogs' legs?

In their panic the peasants joined in the fun and attacked the homes of wealthy land-owners, stealing all their contents and even murdering their animals. Best of all, they burned all the books in which were recorded the rents that they'd been paying (or not). Things were well out of control.

On 27th July, the King ordered the First and Second Estates to join the National Assembly, thinking that this would make the peasants happy. It didn't! They'd got the whiff of revolution in their nostrils – they wanted blood and action and no soppy Assembly was going to stop them. *Sacré bleu* – did this mean the Assembly had lost control too?

Louis Backs Off

The army, as you can imagine, were really not to be relied upon to crush the Revolution and so poor old Louis had to eat humble pie and try to strike a deal with the rebels of the rough, tough National Assembly. Although they still basically wanted a monarchy, the Assembly were dead suspicious of this particular king and reckoned they could go it alone. Rowdy mobs aren't usually that good at organizing governments (see New Labour again) and the Assembly were no exception – but, oh boy, did they have a good go.

On 4th August 1789 the National Assembly tried to make things better for the poor peasants. First they abolished the filthy feudal system which had been punishing the peasants since the Middle Ages (see that fine book, *Middle Ages*, by . . . er, me!) which meant an end to tithes and quite a bit of the power of the nobility and clergy. Then they announced a Declaration of the Rights of Man and the Citizen, which basically told everyone what their new government was all about and promised freedom to all (sounds like New Labour yet again). 'All men are born free and equal in rights', it said. (If you believe that, you'll believe anything.)

Best of all, it made all the rich people from the First and Second Estates pay taxes like the poor had been doing for ages. Things were really moving. Next, Louis was made to accept a Constitution which effectively restricted his power and meant that he was no longer an absolute monarch – poor king.

Time for Action

All this was very well, but in 1789, new government or no new government, France was still well up the creek without a paddle – economically speaking. People were starving on the streets and they wanted action . . . quick action! Louis was well nervous and, reading the writing on the wall, tried in 1791 to escape with Marie and the kids to join the noble *emigrés* abroad, but was caught and dragged back home to the Palace of Versailles (not a bad home to be dragged back to, I might add).

Marie Joseph Paul Yves Roche Gilbert Motier, Marquis de Lafayette*

This French general, statesman and fabulously rich person fought with the Americans in their War of Independence, before returning to France to become a member of the Assembly of Notables, and later of the States General. When the Bastille fell in 1789, he was made commander of the French National Guard, which was created to back up the Assembly's laws. He personally tried to protect the king and queen from the mobs that attacked Versailles, basically because he was a staunch enemy of the extremist Jacobins who were to play a major part in the Revolution. Lafayette very much wanted the King to have a future in France. He finally had to run away, like many counter-Revolutionaries, but was arrested and imprisoned in Austria.

* Sounds more like a menu than a name! Ed

Girl Power

On October 5th 1789 things came to a head when a gaggle of starving Parisian women marched to meet the king at Versailles. They demanded fast food* and that Louis and his

SIX CHEESEBURGERS — AND QUICK!

family be kept at the more central Tuileries Palace where an eye could be kept on them. Louis was well frightened and quickly called in a bit of foreign help, not to mention all those French noblemen who'd been abroad, busy raising armies to help save the monarchy (and the royal family's precious necks). But those particular foreign powers had problems of their own at home and wouldn't come.

Before anything else could happen, a mob broke into the Tuileries, where Louis and his family were staying (Bed & Breakfast only), slaughtered the 600 Swiss Guards (who must have misplaced their little army knives), all the servants and then dragged the king and his family off to a prison called The

* Shouldn't that read 'food fast'? Ed.

Temple, informing Louis that from that point on he was officially unemployed. Things really weren't going that well for Louis, all things considered.

Bad Jobs in Revolutionary France

It certainly wasn't the time to be a Swiss Guard. During the raid the palace was searched from top to bottom by the frenzied mob and many of the guards were thrown from the high windows, while others were butchered on the spot or hacked to pieces by pikes (well, men holding pikes) in the courtyards as they begged for mercy.

Useless Fact No. 769

Small boys played football with the Guards' severed heads in the courtyard (bless 'em), while fearful women cut off more intimate parts of their bodies and ran around waving them in the air. I bet that makes your eyes water, lads.

Oddly enough, many of the aristocrats in Paris took this as a signal to quietly pack their bags and slip away, trying to avoid being spotted by the mob. Those that were recognized at the gates were thrown into prison without any form of trial, to await their fate.

Invasion Time

Very much wanting to see the French monarchy back on the scene, just in case their own personal peasants got any similar ideas, the foreign powers thought the time was now right to invade and so, in the summer of 1792, Prussian armies began crossing the borders and heading for Paris. This made the common folk hate their ex-king even more for getting them into such an awful fix. The new Revolutionary Government, led by Georges Jacques Danton (the minister of justice), rushed every available man out to stop them, while everyone back in Paris had a darned good panic.

Useless Fact No. 772

Danton, a country boy, had good reason to leave his grandfather's farm and come to the city. He had a hideously twisted lip due to getting on the wrong side of an angry bull while sucking the teat of a cow as a boy (weird or what!), a squashed-in nose, due to a replay with said bull, and a host of scars on his cheeks and eyelids caused by being trampled by a herd of runaway pigs. The rest of him was covered by the effects of smallpox. Perhaps someone was trying to tell him something! (Like, get out of farming.)

Chapter 6

THE SEPTEMBER MASSACRES

WARNING:
THIS CHAPTER IS NOT FOR THE SQUEAMISH!!!

Oh dear, oh dear, this is where it gets just a little unpleasant. Where were we? Ah yes! The king had been relieved of all his duties, the huge Prussian army was in French territory threatening to restore Louis and 'severely punish' (i.e. execute) anyone who'd had anything to do with the Revolution (even the dinner ladies). In Paris, the 'aristos', (as they were labelled) that had tried to escape were now, men, women and kids, languishing in the already over-crowded and deeply disgusting prisons.

ARE WE ARISTOS MAMAN?

Suddenly the panicking Revolutionary hordes weren't quite so sure they were doing the right thing.

But another journalist called Jean Paul Marat and the horribly ugly ex-lawyer Danton told them not to be so silly and urged them to hunt out and punish all those who weren't that crazy about the Revolution, which they proceeded, forthwith, to do. They arrested hundreds of people who had voiced any doubt, including most of the priests, but this wasn't enough; they wanted blood and meant to get it – in bucketfuls!

Useless Fact No. 774

There's a very famous picture by Jacques-Louis David called 'Death of Marat' which shows Marat dead in his bath. Isn't it a coincidence that he was killed while he was having his portrait done?*

Massacre Ahoy

Anyway, somehow the hordes got it into their heads that, because there were a few counter-Revolutionaries in the parish prisons, all prisoners must be against the Revolution. They therefore proceeded to attack the scarcely defended prisons on the 2nd September 1792.

Here's a list of some the things they did. If you are of a nervous disposition, might I suggest that you put the book down and go watch the Tellytubbies.**

Six clergymen who refused to join the Revolutionaries were just about to go through the gates of the Abbaye prison in their carriages, when the leader of a Revolutionary mob rushed up and thrust his sabre through the open window and waved it about a bit. His dripping sword was a signal for

---

* I think Monsieur David might just have painted the picture of Marat's assassination sometime later. Ed

** I reckon the Tellytubbies are far more scary. Ed

the others to attack the carriages, severing the limbs of the poor men of God until blood poured onto the cobbled street. The remainder then escaped to a nearby church but were dragged out and slaughtered in the graveyard (convenient, eh!). Their bodies were thrown down a well and their skeletons were discovered some 70 years later.

DING DONG BELL-
VICARS IN THE
WELL

A bunch of Revolutionaries burst into the Carmelite Convent where 150 priests had been held prisoner for a few weeks. The Archbishop fell to his knees, begging for mercy and was slashed across the face by a sword. As he fell to the ground a pike was thrust through his chest. Ouch.

One prisoner tried to escape up the chimney so the jailer, knowing he'd get it if the man got away, shot his musket up into the void. This apparently failed, so he lit a fire and when the asphyxiated man fell into the hearth in a cloud of soot and smoke, he was finished off with swords and hatchets.

Many of the prisons were for men and women convicted of civil crimes – nothing whatsoever to do with politics, let alone the Revolution. There were also those that held female prisoners, and hospitals for the poor and mad. Gangs of citizens broke in with any weapons that came to hand and set about them, pausing every now and again to eat and drink wine, using the mutilated bodies as tables and chairs. Murdering's a thirsty business by all accounts.

Sometimes the intruders would hold drunken mock trials which lasted only minutes and always ended with the 'plaintiff' being dragged from the room and stabbed to death – without so much as a last request.

At the Conciergerie, which held a load of prisoners awaiting trial, 378 out of the 488 prisoners were hacked to pieces and piled in bloody, twitchy heaps. As the carts carrying the corpses away were loaded, some of the women who were helping stopped every now and again to dance amongst the slippery bodies.

Worst of all (and now's the time to hold your breath) was the story of Marie-Antoinette's best friend, the kind and sweet Princesse de Lamballe, who'd been languishing in a prison called La Petite Force. First, she was killed. So far so bad . . . Then, one of her legs was chopped off and fired out of a cannon. (Why?)
Worst of all (if you're a
vegetarian), her heart was
torn out, cooked over an

open fire and eaten. (I've always hated French food . . .) Her highly coiffed head was then stuck on a pike and paraded below her chum Marie-Antoinette's window (who fainted for the first and last time in her life).

There were, apparently, even worse things than that, but it's getting near to supper-time and I'm feeling a little queasy.*

All in all it was estimated that a mob of 150 men massacred 1400 people, only a small percentage of whom had anything to do with the Revolution.

* And I won't allow any more anyway. Ed

Chapter 7

BACK TO THE PLOT

Rather surprisingly, the Revolutionary French Army beat the Prussians at the Battle of Valmy in 1792 (which must have alarmed poor Louis and wife no end) and even won a few more scraps, which extended France's borders far into Belgium. High on success, they then formed a new government called 'The Convention' which kicked off the beginning of the French Republic by simply re-stating that they didn't want the king any more. In fact, they didn't want *any* king any more. In fact, they didn't want this particular king to even be alive any more.

Saint-Just

The Jacobin, Antoine Saint-Just, a right smoothie by all accounts, said there wasn't even a need for a trial – simply being a king was crime enough, which I think is a bit strong. Louis XVI, he said, should be executed right away. Maximilien Robespierre, one of the leaders of the Revolution, agreed with him, claiming that bringing the king to trial would probably bring the Revolution to trial as well. I suppose *he* knew what he was talking about.

Useless Fact No. 777

In November 1792 the French government, cocky with success, offered to help anyone else in Europe if they fancied a revolution of their very own: a kind of Rent-a-Revolution. They called this the Edict of Fraternity. The generals were ordered to take away the property of all the rich people in the lands they conquered, and to end all forms of feudalism. Nice of 'em.

Killing a King

On 11th December 1792, a trial, for want of a better word, actually began. Louis was accused of plotting against the French nation (*very* likely) and helping the Prussian invasion. The king, who knew full well that the whole thing was a farce, accepted his fate and said . . . not a lot. He also knew that his subjects hated his beloved queen far more than they hated him and that to a certain extent he was carrying the can – or rather, her can (or maybe the Can-Can?*). Louis and Marie-Antoinette spent their last night together but their children were sent away. Presumably, having your mum and dad executed (don't try this at home) was thought to be a bit too horrid for even the average French royal *enfant* to bear.

YIPPEE! WE'RE GOING AWAY FOR THE WEEKEND!

* Don't be silly. *Ed*

Louis was beheaded in front of a vast, jolly crowd at the Place de la Révolution in Paris. When his head had been shown to the masses, they fought to buy tiny bundles of hair, or bits of his clothing, from the executioner (a perk of the job), and scrambled to dip pieces of paper, scraps of cloth or just the odd finger into his blood. Someone even tasted it and called it 'vilely salty'. Louis' body (minus head) was put in a wicker basket in the middle of the square and everyone had a huge, drunken party around him.

Not everyone gets to attend their own funeral party – wearing their head or not.

Nice or Not Nice?
Robespierre was essentially quite a nice chap (if you don't mind cruel, megalomaniac revolutionaries) who believed in the goodness of other men. He also reckoned that society could only progress if given its freedom (although history has always proved otherwise*). That was the good side. But he was also a fanatic and would commit the most horrendous crimes in his attempts to do what he considered the right thing. He felt he had to lead 'the Terror' (next chapter) because he was scared of what might happen to his precious Revolution if he didn't. Robespierre, bless 'im, seriously thought that it would one day make France a better place (even if he did have to eliminate half of the population *en route*).

Hébertist ou Indulgent?
Other factions included the Hébertists (led by a real sweetie called René Hébert, who thought the whole business a bit slow and wanted to increase the rate of executions) and the

---

* You almost sound like you know what you're talking about. *Ed*

Indulgents (led by Danton and Desmoulins, who preferred to calm things down a bit). By this time Robespierre hated both of these factions and jumped at the opportunity to run the rabid and runaway Revolution himself.

The Hébertists soon got the chop, as Robespierre accused them of being in league with foreign plotters (rotters!). Within days Hébert and his 18 mates were parted from their heads. Madame Guillotine had struck again.

FASTER

SLOWER

Useless Fact No. 780

The guillotine was invented by Dr Joseph Guillotin (what a coincidence!), a kindly man (oddly enough), who thought that executions should be over as quick as possible (the axe was so terribly hit-and-miss, don't you know). He perfected it by practising on corpses from the morgue (who rarely complained). His new-fangled guillotine never failed to have one's head off in one. During the Revolution, it became affectionately known as Madame Guillotine.

Chapter 8

THE TERROR!

The period that followed, between 1793 and 1795, was called the Reign of Terror. Danton had thrown out a challenge to all the countries desperate to get at the French. It went like this:

> *'The kings in alliance try to intimidate us.*
> *We hurl at their feet,*
> *as a gage of battle,*
> *the French king's head.'*

In other words: 'Watch it! We mean business.'

Brave, admittedly, but seriously asking for it, if you ask me. By March 1793, France was at war with Austria, Prussia, Spain, Sardinia (big deal), Britain and Holland, who'd all joined together to trash the Republic for killing their King Louis.

Heaven knows what right Britain had to have a go at France. We'd topped our King Charles I in our very own revolution only a couple of hundred years before. (See my brilliant book, *Roundheads and Cavaliers*.*)

Plots a-Plenty

On top of all that, there were lots of plots to overthrow the Revolution from within France, led by noblemen who'd been forced out of the country. They worked with the foreigners to

* You haven't written it yet. Ed
Details, details! JF

try to get France back and even shipped emigrant French soldiers back in to head a counter-revolution.

By the end of 1793, however, the Revolutionaries had won just about every stage of the battle and the threat of invasion had passed. Meantime, within the National Convention (*le Parlement* of 1791), several splinter groups formed and arguments soon broke out between the different factions – the moderate Girondins and the grumpy but cleverer Jacobins, who included Danton and Robespierre. A Committee of Public Safety was set up in order to deal with the crisis, controlled by Robespierre and the Jacobins. In 1793 the bizarre and sneaky 'Law of Parial' was set up, which meant that they could convict people without bothering with evidence, followed by a wicked 'Law of Suspects', which allowed people to be locked up without the tedious and time-wasting process of a trial.

I Love Paris

Paris, during the days of the Terror, was certainly not the place to go for that romantic little weekend break. It's difficult to imagine, while strolling through those beautiful streets, that such horrors could possibly have occurred.

It all started with the execution of Queen Marie-Antoinette. She'd been kept in a tiny, cold, damp, dark cell accused of all sorts of crimes.

Chic Marie

Being the stylish lady that she was, she made sure she looked really nice for her execution – in a white dress, white hat, black stockings and red high-heeled shoes.

I'LL LOOK SIMPLY DREADFUL WITH NO HEAD

Useless Fact No. 784

After the customary haircut (to bare the neck) she was ushered into the courtyard to the waiting cart. She was so nervous that she was forced to have a pee in the corner of the courtyard in front of everyone, which is not much fun if you're a queen.*

Useless Fact No. 787

As she climbed onto the scaffold, Marie-Antoinette trod on the executioner's foot. Her apology turned out to be the last words she ever spoke. The executioner graciously accepted her apology and then, without further ado, chopped her head off.

Chop Chop!

From then on the guillotine's razor-sharp blade was to rise and fall like a conductor's baton. One of the more famous of the early executions was that of the Mayor of Paris, Jean-Silvain Bailly. As he walked to his doom, the crowds threw mud, spat

* It's not a lot of fun if you're not a queen. Ed

in his face and kicked him. It really wasn't his day: the execution took place on a dunghill on the banks of the Seine and the mobs howled with joy to see him die.

These executions gradually increased to a steady flow throughout the later half of 1793 as unsuccessful military leaders, politicians from the wrong side, writers of articles criticizing the Revolution, even nuns and churchmen, all lost their heads to the extreme elation of the *sans-culottes*. Nearly 3,000 were slaughtered, and anyone who even knew anyone with the slightest cause to worry would lie in bed at night dreading the ominous knock on the front door.

Useless Fact No. 789
The *sans-culottes* was the nickname given to the poorer Revolutionaries and means 'without breeches'.*

By now, anyone with a more than average amount of money, or anyone who'd ever murmured a criticism about the way things were going, was regarded as an enemy and executed. Even poor people, some of whom were accused of hoarding food, or giving evidence badly, or depraving public morals (whatever that means), were taken to a *rendezvous* with the guillotine. The Committee of Public Safety declared that the Terror was necessary to get rid of the Royalists once and for all, and one of its leaders, the cool, cruel Saint-Just, said: 'You must punish not just the traitors, but the indifferent as well.'

* *Sans-culottes* didn't mean that they wore no trousers at all. They just didn't have proper, fastened-at-the-knee trousers, like the rich. Ed

The Net Widens

In the country it was even worse, with some 14,000 losing their heads – eight out of ten of these were not rich but poor. If you weren't actually executed, then you were probably one of those enjoying the spectacle of it being done to someone else – that's human nature for you! Whole families – mum, dad and the kids – went to the guillotine simply for having a distant relative on the wrong side; women for weeping at the death of a father or brother, peasant girls for dancing with Prussian soldiers, even a landlord who served Revolutionaries with poor quality wine; all said a fond farewell to their heads (or bodies?).

THIS WINE TASTES A BIT DODGY

. . . and Widens

Then the net widened still more. Awkward neighbours were reported to the tribunal as counter-Revolutionaries and promptly executed without a shred of evidence; even people with similar names to the already convicted were done just in case they might be guilty.

Speed It Up!

But the guillotine was proving to be a little slow – I mean, you could only do one at a time – and the prisons were becoming a bit overcrowded. Jean Baptist Carrier, the Committee's mad agent at Nantes, had a nasty solution. He took 2,000 prisoners bound together in pairs and without a stitch of clothing, in barges to the middle of the Loire and threw them over the side. After a while the river was choked with rotting human flesh, so much so that even the fish were deemed unfit to eat. Carrier became obsessed with the power of killing people, especially children, and especially picked on anyone who pleaded for their salvation.

Elsewhere they had other methods of getting rid of people quickly. At one place, over 300 poor souls were taken out to a field, bound together by rope, shot by cannon and finished off with muskets.

It was a kind of fever, and the blood-crazed judges competed with each other to see who could be the most barbaric. One poor woman, seen weeping at the execution of her husband, was forced to sit for hours under the blade, so that the blood from the headless corpse would gradually drip all over her. She was then executed herself.

Family Fun

Meanwhile, the executions in Paris became a treat for all those whose name hadn't yet come up. There were rows of seats around the scaffold at la Place de la Révolution and cheeky street vendors wove amongst the expectant crowds selling food and wine. There were the famous old women called *tricoteuses* (French for 'knitters'), who sat knitting throughout the fun, only raising their eyes on hearing the thud of the blade, so they could watch the heads rolling into the baskets.

The laughing, drunken crowds would place bets on the order of executions, and turn round excitedly to see who was arriving in the constant stream of tumbrils (carts) that rattled along the cobbles of the Rue Saint-Honoré into the square – which by now reeked to high heaven of aristocratic (and other) blood.

. . . and Widens Again

But the net was *still* widening. Not only were they after the rich clerics of the First Estate, but there was also a backlash against anything Christian. Churches were looted and destroyed and their ministers arrested. Streets with Christian-sounding names were renamed and all church festivals were cancelled. Priests (who'd taken a vow of celibacy) were ordered to either marry, adopt a child or look after an elderly person. I think I'd have preferred execution!*

---

* I think I believe you. Ed

Crazy Calendar

Sundays were no longer to be a day of rest. They even replaced the Gregorian calendar (the one we use now) with one of their own. There were to be 12 months of 30 days each and the remaining five days were to be called, ludicrously, *sans-culottides,* which were festivals (festivals without trousers?). A little later, all churches were ordered to be closed and turned into Temples of Reason (how unreasonable), and a huge, very silly Festival of Reason, in praise of the Revolution, was held at Nôtre Dame. In Paris, people danced and sang in the streets, and, reminiscent of the Festival of No Trousers, many of the men disported themselves bare below the waist while many of the women were bare above it. They even carried out 'lewd acts' in the shadows of the chapels and churches.

But France was, underneath it all, a very religious country and there was a huge undercurrent of fear and anger at such blasphemies. What next?

Chapter 9

ROBESPIERRE DUCKS OUT

Robespierre realized that in order to be in complete charge he'd have to get rid of the much more popular Danton and his fans, which was easier said than done. But eventually they were all arrested, swiftly tried and executed. Robespierre was now head *homme;* he believed that, together with his sidekicks, Saint-Just, Couthon and Hanriot, he could at last direct the Revolution onto a virtuous course with the support of the *sans-culottes.* The public had become fed up with the killings and whole areas of Paris had begun to stink like an abattoir. Not only that, but it had been a long time since only the rich lost contact with their heads. By now 80% of the headless were from the ranks of the poor, and the idle gossip on the street corners was mostly about who was to be next.

All His Fault

Predictably, Robespierre was eventually blamed, not only for the carnage, but also for whipping up all the troubles. At the Convention he had to listen to a whole list of his crimes against the state but was refused permission to speak (a dose of his own medicine). In the end, he rushed up and down yelling 'Death, death' at his accusers; not a very good move in such circumstances. Robespierre and his chums were eventually arrested, charged, found guilty and frog-marched (how appropriate*) from the Assembly to the Hôtel de Ville (town

---

* It's rude to call the French 'frogs'. Ed
Why? They call us 'roast beefs'. JF

hall). At this time nobody was quite sure who were patriots and who weren't. Robespierre, bless 'im, was still certain that his captors would see the error of their ways and put him back in charge. But it all started to go even wronger.

Trouble Ahead

The Hôtel de Ville was being taken over by Robespierre's enemies. Just as he was about to sign what was called an 'Appeal to Arms', one of them pulled out a gun and shot him in the face, shattering his jaw. Robespierre then leapt up and flung himself out of the window. Bad move – he'd forgotten he was several floors up. So, to add to his problems, he broke one of his legs. Later that day he and 21 of his mates were taken to la Place de la Révolution along a route lined by cheering, jeering, blood-lusty Parisians. Just as they arrived, a woman broke from the mob, yelling: 'You monster . . . go down into your grave burdened with the curses of the wives and mothers of France . . . The thought of your execution makes me drunk with joy.' I don't think she cared for him much, do you?

Robespierre and co. must have looked a bizarre sight. The boss was hideously disfigured and wearing a blood-soaked bandage; Hanriot, his collaborator, had been thrown out of the same window, onto a dunghill, and his eye was hanging out of

its socket due to an argument with a soldier's bayonet; Couthon, an invalid, had plunged down the stairs head-first in his wheelchair, and banged his head at the bottom. Only the smarmy Saint-Just was still immaculate from head to foot. Just as they were about to be executed, a bystander jumped forward and nicked poor Hanriot's hanging eye as a souvenir. Not to be outdone, Robespierre tore off the bandage holding his jaw in place and let the blood pour out of the wound. But the execution went ahead and with it went the extremist Jacobin stranglehold on the Revolution. Although nobody realized it at the time, the Terror, that had accounted for so many lives, was finally over.

Chapter 10

AFTER THE REVOLUTION OR: OUT OF THE FRYING PAN . . .

After the death of Robespierre, and the demise of the Jacobins, the moderates, who were now running the Convention, stamped their authority on the Committee of Public Safety. There was an enormous feeling of relief that the Reign of Terror was over, but this relief soon turned to anger when they thought of all the blood that had been shed so pointlessly. Everyone fell over themselves claiming that they'd had nothing to do with it (just like the Germans and most of occupied Europe after the Holocaust). But the Jacobins weren't just out of the frame politically – they were running for their lives from all those who had suffered at their hands, or had lost members of their families to the infamous Madame Guillotine. This witch-hunt became known as the 'White Terror', especially in the South of France.

Free at Last
For a time Paris revelled under its new freedom. Clothes became extravagant and over the top, smart restaurants (for

SORRY MONSIEUR-HAVE YOU RESERVED A TABLE?

those that still had heads with mouths to put food in) opened again, and all those with money went back to having a swell time. Gambling clubs and theatres sprang up everywhere and a new passion for dancing emerged. And from February 1795 everyone became free to worship whatever God they liked best.

Useless Fact No. 792

Most famous of all the dances were the *bals des victimes*: parties thrown by those that had lost friends or rellies to the guillotine during the Terror. The revellers wore thin braids of red silk round their necks representing the axeman's mark, and cut their hair short at the back, like their nearest and dearest had done when about to have their heads chopped off.

Trouble Again

But the poor or *sans-culottes* were to have no rest. There was a horribly severe winter in 1794 and the crops failed resulting in yet another severe shortage of bread. The Convention, consisting of the rich and powerful, fearing another revolution (a revolution *against* the Revolution), sent for the soldiers to crush the demonstrations before they got out of hand. Just to be on the safe side, 3–4,000 people were flung into jail. Old habits die hard, I suppose.

Power was then handed over to five men called the Directory who more or less ruled France and tried to bring it back to some sort of economic stability. Unfortunately, the now out-from-under-the-table Royalists, who wanted a nice King Louis again, weren't too thrilled and plotted their downfall. The Directory relied on the powerful army to keep this lot at bay. But things weren't over yet.

Chapter 11

GRAND FINALE

17th Louis?

The Royalists were getting rather excited about bringing Louis XVI's son, Louis (surprise, surprise) to the throne but he caught tuberculosis (some say he was poisoned) in the cold, damp Temple prison, where he died, aged 10.

18th Louis?

Within a month, an army arrived from Britain to try and put the chap who would have been Louis XVIII, the former Compte de Provence, on the throne, but the Revolutional Army was too powerful and the Convention weren't yet in the mood for a restoration of the monarchy: 750 men died in the attempt. The Royalists' cause was dashed, but not for long.

Napoleon!

In October 1795 a Royalist uprising of 25,000 people in Paris caught everyone on the hop. The Convention quickly called all their troops to arms. One of these was a young general called . . . Napoleon Bonaparte (who you just might have heard of). But that, I'm afraid, is another story.*

PARDON, MES AMIS—
BUT APPARENTLY
I'M ANOTHER
STORY!

* And, I'm delighted to say, you've run out of words. Ed

⬱ *TIME'S UP*

How are you feeling after that little lot? Ready for your dinner? I bet you didn't think that those smart, sophisticated Frenchies were capable of such horrors – and only a couple of hundred years ago.

If you want even more gruesome detail (sicko!) then you'll find plenty in your local library. As for me, I've had enough and I've got to get on with the next book. If you want to start saving up your pocket money for it now, it should take you just about as long as it will take me to write it – unless your parents are *real* meanies!

JOHN FARMAN
HISTORY IN A HURRY
Very good, very short, very funny
(and very cheap).

Ancient China	0 330 37087 1	£1.99
Ancient Egypt	0 330 35248 2	£1.99
Ancient Greece	0 330 35249 0	£1.99
Aztecs	0 330 35247 4	£1.99
Dark Ages	0 330 37086 3	£1.99
French Revolution	0 330 37089 8	£1.99
Middle Ages	0 330 35252 0	£1.99
Romans	0 330 35250 4	£1.99
Stuarts	0 330 37088 X	£1.99
Tudors	0 330 35251 2	£1.99
Victorians	0 330 35253 9	£1.99
Vikings	0 330 35254 7	£1.99

All Macmillan titles can be ordered at your local
bookshop or are available by post from:

Book Service by Post
PO Box 29, Douglas, Isle of Man IM99 1BQ

Credit cards accepted. For details:
Telephone: 01624 675137
Fax: 01624 670923
E-mail: bookshop@enterprise.net

Free postage and packing in the UK.
Overseas customers: add £1 per book (paperback)
and £3 per book (hardback).

The prices shown are correct at the time of going to press. However,
Macmillan Publishers reserve the right to show new retail prices on covers
which may differ from those previously advertised.